You Are Not Broken:

Tools to Overcome Trauma & Thrive

Georgina Twumasi

ISBN: 978-1-955312-75-2

Printed in the United States of America

Story Corner Publishing & Consulting, Inc.

Chesapeake, VA 23321

Storycornerpublishing@yahoo.com

www.StoryCornerPublishing.com

Table of Contents

INTRODUCTION

Starting over can be hard, but it is not impossible. We all go through different journeys in different chapters of our lives. Do not rush the process but embrace every moment of it. There is always a lesson to learn. Every model is generally the same. There is trauma or abuse on one end and healing on the other, but no one really talks about what happens in between. In the middle, a death of some sort takes place, but it is a unique death which varies one person to the next. You will then notice the five stages of grief according to the Kübler-Ross model, which are denial, anger, bargaining, depression, and acceptance. I found myself in each of these stages fighting for my life in the middle. Before I became healed, many things in my life had to die like trauma bounds, generational curses, toxic thinking, codependency, low self-esteem, pride, bitterness, resentment, abandonment, neglect, rejection, childhood trauma, negative speech, etc. I had to embrace the road to recovery. I have children who look up to me anddepend on me. Most importantly I needed healing and wholeness for myself.

In this workbook, you will have a chance to write down any questions, concerns, and thoughts. Writing is an important part of healing because this type of therapy enables you to release things in private until you can talk it over with someone. You have the chance to tell your truth without feeling fear or judgment. After you have released it on paper, it will give your mind more freedom to process what happened to you. Then I would suggest you pray about the situation and ask God to heal you. God can perform a miraculous healing for you, or He may give you steps to follow. Keep in mind everyone's healing process is different and every process has its own turnaround time. The most important part is that you start the process and do not stop until it is finished. Whatever steps God gives you, just obey even if it seems crazy. He does want the best for His people.

I just want to say that I am proud of you for getting this far in your process. Taking the first step is the hardest, but once you accomplish that it only gets easier with every step thereafter. I have been there and can only give you something I had to live through. I made it and I have hope and faith that you will too. You can do this! Remember, fear only comes to stop and block you but do it afraid anyway! Freedom is only a plan away.

WELCOME!

My name is Georgina Twumasi and I am a devoted mother and woman of faith in God. Family and building emotional wealth are the pillars of my success. I am no stranger to life transitions, having relocated to the United States from Ghana in my youth. I overcame many obstacles which got me to where I am today. I am a psychiatric APRN and founder of "Psych on Demand," located in multiple locations of Connecticut. Good mental health is one of the keys to unraveling many of our sufferings. As a nurse practitioner, holistic healing for the mind, body, and soul is my area of expertise. I have over ten years of experience working with both inpatient and outpatient procedures. I am here to serve you in any way that I can. Together we can accomplish extraordinary things! Let's continue to take the necessary steps to thrive. A better tomorrow awaits you on the other side of your healing journey.

CHAPTER 1

WORKING THROUGH CODEPENDENCY

"You Are Not Broken: Tools to Overcome Trauma & Thrive," focuses on understanding and addressing codependent thought patterns through cognitive behavioral techniques, self-esteem- building exercises, and attachment styles. Participants will enhance body awareness through self- care practices, assertive body language, and writing therapy. Spiritual practices, such as fasting, will help release blame, shame, and guilt, and seek divine guidance for healthier relationships. Causes of codependency include trauma, adverse life experiences, attachment styles, complicated family relationships, and cultural and social factors.

MIND

Identifying and Addressing Codependent Thought Patterns

Notes:

Recognizing thoughts that prioritize others' needs over your own and create a sense of obligation.

Examples: Common thoughts include feeling responsible for another's happiness or believing you must "fix" them.

Action: Use mindfulness to notice these thoughts and challenge their validity by asking if they are rational or helpful.

Reflect on any thoughts or beliefs you have that prioritize others' needs over your own. How do these thoughts impact your well-being and relationships?

_____
_____
_____
_____
_____

Questions:

- How can mindfulness help in recognizing and addressing codependent thought patterns?

_____
_____
_____
_____
_____

- What strategies can you use to challenge and reframe negative codependent beliefs?

_____
_____
_____
_____
_____

Self-Esteem Building Exercises

Notes:

Low self-esteem is often at the core of codependency. Building self-esteem is crucial for recovery.

Practices

- Make a list of your positive qualities and accomplishments.
- Set small, achievable goals and celebrate meeting them.
- Practice self-compassion and positive self-talk.
- Engage in activities that make you feel confident and capable.
- Spend time with supportive people who appreciate you.

List three of your positive qualities and recent accomplishments. How do these attributes contribute to your self-esteem?

_____
_____
_____
_____
_____

Questions:

- What are some small, achievable goals you can set for yourself to build confidence?

_____
_____
_____
_____
_____

- How can practicing self-compassion and positive self-talk improve your self-esteem?

Affirmations for Codependency Recovery

Notes:
Positive affirmations can help rewire codependent thought patterns and reinforce self-worth.

Examples:

1. "I am worthy of love and respect, just as I am."
2. "My needs and feelings are valid and important."
3. "I trust myself to make good decisions."

Choose an affirmation that resonates with you and write about how it reflects your journey toward recovery from codependency.

_____

_____

_____

_____

_____

Questions:

- Which affirmation do you find most meaningful, and why?

_____

_____

_____

_____

_____

_____

- How can repeating positive affirmations daily support your recovery process?

_____

_____

_____

_____

_____

Attachment Styles

Attachment style refers to the way individuals form emotional bonds and connections with others based on early experiences with caregivers. These attachment styles can affect individuals' mental health and relationship dynamics.

Four Attachment Styles:

1. Secure: The healthiest form of attachment. These are people who are comfortable expressing emotions in a relationship, are comfortable with closeness, and are not fearful within a relationship. They're capable of being in relationships that are characterized by mutual regard and reciprocity—they don't need a relationship to feel complete.

2. Ambivalent (Anxious): Feeling insecure in close relationships-often devaluing yourself and overvaluing the other person. There is a chronic fear of abandonment in their relationships, and they often require contact and reassurance to feel safe.

3. Avoidant (Dismissive): A person with an avoidant attachment style will want and need a loving connection with another person but will not trust that this person won't hurt or reject them. This person won't share deep feelings nor vulnerability and will pull away when the other person gets too close.

4. Disorganized (Fearful Avoidant): A combination of the anxious and avoidant styles. This person will exhibit strong emotions of needing, and then rejecting. This attachment style is marked by being so afraid that the other person will leave that they'll often leave first.

What was your childhood like?

_____

_____

_____

What kind of parents did/do you have?

_____

_____

_____

Questions:

- What attachment style do you think you display in relationships? Why?

_____

_____

_____

- On a scale of 1 to 10, how well do you trust others?

_____

- Do you share your deep feelings with others easily? Do you welcome support from others?

_____

_____

- According to your attachment style, how do you think you can improve yourself and your relationships in a healthy manner?

_____

_____

_____

_____

BODY

Self-Care Practices for Co-dependent Individuals

Self-care helps build a sense of self-worth and autonomy.

Practices

- Regular Exercise: Engage in physical activities you enjoy for at least 30 minutes a day.
- Balanced Nutrition: Plan meals with a variety of fruits, vegetables, lean proteins, and whole grains.
- Adequate Sleep: Establish a regular sleep routine, aiming for 7-9 hours per night.
- Relaxation Techniques: Practice deep breathing, progressive muscle relaxation, or other calming techniques.
- Joyful Activities: Pursue hobbies or activities that make you happy.
- Regular Health Check-ups: Schedule regular appointments with healthcare providers.

Describe your current self-care routine. How does it support your physical and emotional well-being?

_____

_____

_____

_____

_____

_____

Questions:

- What changes can you make to your self-care routine to better support your recovery from codependency?

_____

_____

_____

_____

- How do regular exercise, balanced nutrition, and adequate sleep contribute to building self-worth and autonomy?

_____

_____

_____

_____

_____

SPIRIT

Spiritual Practices for Releasing Blame, Shame, and Guilt

Spiritual practices can help release negative emotions and foster self- compassion.

Examples:

- Self-Forgiveness: Engage in daily meditation or prayer focused on self- forgiveness.
- Affirmations: Use positive affirmations to counter negative self-talk.
- Journaling: Write about feelings of blame, shame, and guilt.
- Study: Read (Ephesians 4:32, Colossians 3:13, Matthew 6:14-15, Luke 6:37) on forgiveness and self-compassion.

Write about a recent experience where you practiced self-forgiveness or used affirmations. How did these practices affect your mindset and emotions?

_____

_____

_____

_____

_____

Questions:

- What role do spiritual practices play in overcoming feelings of blame, shame, and guilt?

_____

_____

_____

_____

- How can studying scriptures Hebrews 10:24-25, Isaiah 53:5, and Psalm 103:2-3 support your healing journey?

_____

_____

_____

_____

Physical Boundaries and Body Awareness Exercises

Establishing physical boundaries and increasing body awareness helps recognize and respect your physical space and needs.

Practices

- Assertive body language: Stand tall, make eye contact, and use open body language.
- Role-playing: Practice saying "no" in firm but polite language.
- Mindfulness: Engage in body scan meditations and mindful movement.

- Grounding techniques: Press your feet into the ground or hold a comforting object.

Reflect on a recent situation where you needed to set a physical boundary. How did you handle it, and what did you learn from the experience?

_____

_____

_____

_____

_____

Questions:

- How can practicing assertive body language and physical boundaries enhance your sense of autonomy?

_____

_____

_____

_____

_____

- What mindfulness or grounding techniques have you found effective in reconnecting with your body and needs?

_____

_____

_____

_____

_____

Writing Therapy for Codependency

Writing therapy helps articulate thoughts and feelings, fostering self- awareness and healing.

Practices

- Keep a body-focused journal to track stress levels and self-care activities.
- Write letters to your body to foster a compassionate relationship.
- Engage in expressive writing for 20 minutes to explore feelings related to codependency.
- Create a self-care plan outlining actions for physical health and review it regularly.

Engage in expressive writing for 20 minutes about your experiences and feelings related to codependency. Reflect on what you discovered about yourself through this exercise.

_____
_____
_____
_____
_____
_____
_____
_____
_____

Questions:

- How can writing therapy help you process and heal from codependency?

_____
_____
_____
_____

- What specific self-care actions can you include in your plan to support your recovery?

_____

_____

_____

_____

_____

Seeking God for Healthy Relationships

Seeking God can help in establishing and maintaining healthy relationships.

- Develop a regular prayer or meditation practice focused on relationship guidance.
- Practice mindfulness to become more aware of your needs and boundaries.

Describe your experience with any spiritual practices used for relationship guidance. How have these practices influenced your approach to relationships?

_____

_____

_____

_____

_____

_____

_____

Questions:

- In what ways can seeking God help improve your relationships?

_____

_____

_____

- How can mindfulness and contemplative practices contribute
  to understanding and honoring your needs in relationships?

_____

_____

_____

_____

CHAPTER 2

RECOVERY FROM AN ABUSIVE RELATIONSHIP

Prayer offers a way to connect with GOD, while meditation helps to focus on God's Word and calms the mind. During Weeks 3 and 4, participants will focus on the initial steps of recovery from an abusive relationship. This module is designed to help you understand and begin the healing process by addressing the mind, body, and spirit. Each aspect of your being has been affected by the trauma, and each requires attention and care to facilitate holistic recovery.

MIND

Introduction to Talk Therapy

Notes:

Talk therapy is a crucial component in recovering from an abusive relationship. It provides a safe, confidential space for survivors to process their experiences with a trained professional. This therapy helps individuals understand the impact of abuse, work through trauma, and develop healthier coping mechanisms.

Common Types of Talk Therapy for Abuse Survivors

- Cognitive Behavioral Therapy (CBT): Focuses on changing negative thought patterns.
- Trauma-Focused Therapy: Specifically addresses the effects of abuse.

Reflect on your thoughts about seeking therapy. What fears or hopes do you have?

_____

_____

_____

_____

Questions:

- How do you feel about discussing your experiences with a therapist?

_____

_____

_____

_____

_____

_____

- What qualities would you like in a therapist?

_____

_____

_____

Techniques for Rest & Reset (Clear Mind)

Notes:

Rest and reset techniques help to calm the mind and body, essential for trauma recovery.

Techniques to Try

- Mindfulness Meditation: Focus on the present moment to reduce anxiety.

- Deep Breathing Exercises: Use slow, controlled breathing to activate relaxation.
- Progressive Muscle Relaxation: Tense and relax muscles to release tension.
- Grounding Techniques: Use sensory awareness to connect with the present.

Which technique resonates with you? How can you incorporate it into your daily routine?

_____

_____

_____

_____

_____

Questions:

- How do you feel after practicing these techniques?

_____

_____

_____

_____

_____

- Which technique helps you feel most relaxed?

_____

_____

_____

Positive Thinking and Speaking Exercises

Developing positive thinking patterns is crucial in overcoming a negative self- image often resulting from abuse.

Exercises to Try:

- Affirmations: Short, powerful statements to reshape thought patterns.
- Cognitive Restructuring: Identify and challenge negative thoughts, replacing them with balanced ones.
- Gratitude Practice: Keep a daily gratitude journal to focus on positive aspects of life.

Write down three affirmations you can repeat daily. How do these affirmations make you feel?

_____

_____

_____

_____

_____

Questions:

- What negative thoughts do you struggle with most?

_____

_____

_____

_____

_____

_____

_____

_____

- How can you reframe these thoughts to be more positive?

_____

_____

_____

_____

_____

_____

_____

BODY

Basics of Healthy Eating for Recovery

Proper nutrition plays a crucial role in healing from trauma. Focus on eating regular, balanced meals, incorporating foods rich in omega-3 fatty acids, consuming plenty of fruits and vegetables, staying hydrated, and limiting caffeine and alcohol.

What are some healthy foods you enjoy? How can you include more of these in your diet?

_____

_____

_____

_____

Questions:

- How do your eating habits affect your mood and eating habits?

_____

_____

_____

- What small changes can you make to improve your nutrition?

_____

_____

_____

Introduction to Exercise and Stretching for Trauma Healing

Physical activity helps release tension, reduce stress, and improve overall well-being.

Exercises to Try:

- Low-Impact Activities: Start with walking, swimming, or similar activities.
- Gentle Stretching: Release physical tension stored in the body.
- Mindful Movement: Practice Tai chi or Qigong to connect body and mind.
- Strength Training: Build confidence and body awareness.
- Trauma-Sensitive Classes: Consider classes designed for survivors.

How does your body feel after exercise? What changes do you notice in your mood and energy?

_____
_____
_____

Questions:

- What types of physical activities do you enjoy?

_____
_____
_____

- How can you make exercise a regular part of your routine?

_____
_____
_____

Establishing a Healthy Sleep Routine

Sleep disturbances are common among trauma survivors. Establishing a consistent sleep routine can significantly improve recovery.

Steps to Take:

- Set a regular sleep schedule.
- Create a calming bedtime ritual.
- Use white noise or calming sounds to promote sleep.
- Limit caffeine and avoid heavy meals close to bedtime.

Describe your idea bedtime routine. What helps you feel relaxed before sleeping?

_____

_____

_____

_____

Questions:

- How does your current sleep routine affect your rest?

_____

_____

_____

- What changes can you make to improve your sleep quality?

_____

_____

_____

_____

SPIRIT

Understanding Forgiveness in the Context of Abuse

Forgiveness doesn't mean condoning the abusive behavior or reconciling with the abuser. It's a personal process of letting go of anger and resentment for your own healing.

What does forgiveness mean to you? How do you feel about the idea of forgiving those who have hurt you?

_____

_____

_____

_____

_____

_____

_____

Questions:

- What emotions come up when you think about forgiveness?

_____

_____

_____

- How can forgiveness contribute to your healing process?

_____

_____

_____

_____

Introduction to Prayer and Meditation

Prayer offers a way to connect with a God, while meditation helps calm the mind and increase self-awareness.

Scriptures for Meditation:

- "For I know the plans I have for you..." (Jeremiah 29:11 NIV)
- "And we know that in all things God works for the good..." (Romans 8:28 NIV)
- "No weapon forged against you will prevail..." (Isaiah 54:17 NIV)
- "And my God will meet all your needs..." (Philippians 4:19 NIV)

The Serenity Prayer

God grant me the serenity to accept the things I cannot change; courage to change the things I can; and wisdom to know the difference.

Living one day at a time; Enjoying one moment at a time;

Accepting hardships as the pathway to peace;

Taking, as He did, this sinful world as it is, not as I would have it;

Trusting that He will make all things right if I surrender to His Will;

That I may be reasonably happy in this life and supremely happy with Him

Forever in the next.

Amen.

"The Serenity Prayer" can bring life into a better and clearer perspective if we meditate on the words. When life spins out of control, take a moment to think about the words to this prayer. Hopefully, it will help you to navigate through your situation with

God's wisdom. I pray this prayer helps you to accept the things you cannot change in life and build the courage to change the things you can!

Reflect on how prayer and meditation make you feel. What do you seek from these practices?

_____

_____

_____

_____

_____

Questions:

- How does connecting with God bring you comfort?

_____

_____

_____

_____

_____

- How can you incorporate prayer or meditation into your daily routine?

_____

_____

_____

_____

Daily Self-Examination Practices

Daily self-examination involves reflecting on your thoughts, feelings, and actions. This practice can help in identifying negative thought patterns, recognizing progress in healing, and setting intentions for personal growth

What did you learn about yourself today? How are you progressing in your healing journey?

_____

_____

_____

_____

_____

_____

Questions:

- What areas of your life need more attention? Why?

_____

_____

_____

_____

_____

_____

- How can you use self-examination to support your growth?

_____

_____

_____

_____

Are You New to Relationships?

Red Flags to Watch Out For

- Love bombing
- Moving too quickly
- Not introducing you to their friends or family
- Gaslighting
- Inconsistent behavior

- Ignoring or having a problem with your boundaries
- You don't like their friends
- Recognizing their stories don't add up or spotting a lie
- Guilt-tripping or manipulation
- Silent treatment between conversations
- Harsh jokes that hurt your feelings
- Angry outbursts about small things
- Constantly bringing up their ex
- Having a controlling or disrespectful parent
- Constantly seeking their friend's approval
- Dwelling on traumatic past events
- Frequent negative thinking or speaking
- Jealousy, controlling behavior, or getting physical in a negative manner
- Trauma bonding

Reflect on any red flags you've noticed in past relationships. How can you apply these lessons to future relationships?

_____
_____
_____
_____
_____

Questions:

- What steps can you take to ensure your safety and well-being in future relationships?

_____
_____
_____
_____

- How can you regain your power and move forward in your healing journey?

_____

_____

_____

_____

_____

- There are many red flags we should all avoid while dating, courting, or looking for a significant other. Red flags could include anything from jealousy to trauma bonding. Take a moment to think of some red flags you have experienced. Then note how long you tolerated the red flags before the relationship or situation was over. Why did you tolerate the red flags for so long?

_____

_____

_____

_____

_____

_____

_____

_____

- Now, write down an action plan. Would you change anything during your course of dating, courtship, or "getting to know you" phase? If so, what would it be?

_____

_____

_____

_____

_____

_____

_____

Steps to Recover from Abusive Relationships

1. Acknowledge the abuse

2. Remove the abuser from your life

3. Find support

4. Focus on things that interest you

5. Find a creative outlet

6. Resume or develop a regular schedule

7. Consider a support group

8. Focus on your health

9. Avoid places you may bump into the abuser

10. Take time to heal before entering new relationships

11. Move beyond blame and give yourself grace

12. Forgive and move on

13. Regain your power

14. Avoid continuing the cycle by not becoming like the person who hurt you

Create a list that includes things you like to do along with new things you would like to try.

Don't be shy! Step out on faith and mark it down on your calendar. Do not second guess it, just do it. If you do not like the new thing you tried, it's ok. You created a memory to look back and say you had the courage to try something new.

_____

_____

_____

_____

CHAPTER 3

REJECTING PEOPLE PLEASING

Welcome to Weeks 5 and 6. During these weeks, we will delve into rejecting people-pleasing behaviors by nurturing your mind, body, and spirit. This approach will help you build confidence, assert your needs, and foster healthier relationships.

MIND

Introduction to People-Pleasing

Notes:

People-pleasing involves prioritizing others' needs over your own. Common signs include difficulty saying "no," preoccupation with others' opinions, and neglecting personal needs. Causes often include poor self-esteem, insecurity, perfectionism, and past trauma.

Reflect on a recent situation where you felt compelled to please someone else at your own expense. What were your thoughts and feelings during that time?

_____

_____

_____

_____

Questions:

- What are some common signs of people-pleasing behaviors you've noticed in yourself?

_____
_____
_____
_____

- How do these behaviors impact your relationships and well-being?

_____
_____
_____
_____

Cognitive Techniques to Combat People-Pleasing

Notes:

- Identify negative thought patterns, such as "I must be liked by everyone."
- Challenge and reframe these thoughts to more balanced perspectives.
- Practice behavioral experiments to test the validity of negative thoughts.

Track a recent situation where you had a people-pleasing thought. Write down the thought, challenge its validity, and reframe it into a more balanced perspective.

_____
_____
_____
_____
_____
_____

Questions:

- What are some negative thought patterns associated with people-pleasing that you've identified?

_____

_____

_____

_____

- How can you reframe these thoughts to support a healthier self-image?

_____

_____

_____

_____

Assertiveness Training

- Assertiveness involves clearly expressing needs and boundaries.
- Use "I" statements to communicate your feelings and limits without blaming others.
- Practice role-playing scenarios to build confidence in assertive communication.

Write about a recent situation where you practiced assertiveness. How did it feel to express your needs and set boundaries?

_____

_____

_____

_____

Questions:

- What are some key differences between assertiveness and aggression?

_____

_____

_____

_____

- How can assertiveness training help you reject people-pleasing behaviors?

_____

_____

_____

_____

Positive Self-Talk and Motivation

Replace negative self-talk with positive affirmations.

- Identify and challenge common negative thinking patterns.
- Regularly practice positive self-talk to boost self-esteem and resilience.

Identify a negative thought you often have about yourself. Reframe it using a positive affirmation and reflect on how this change affects your mindset.

_____

_____

_____

_____

_____

_____

Questions:

- What are some examples of negative self-talk you experience?

_____

_____

_____

_____

- How can positive self-talk improve your ability to set boundaries and prioritize yourself?

_____

_____

_____

_____

BODY

Body Language for Assertiveness

- Assertive body language includes good posture, eye contact, and open gestures.
- Practice maintaining a confident stance and using deliberate movements.

Observe and note your body language during interactions. How do your posture and eye contact influence your assertiveness?

_____

_____

_____

_____

Questions:

- What are some signs of assertive body language?

_____

_____

_____

- How can improving your body language impact your ability to set boundaries?

_____

_____

_____

Keep in mind, healthy boundaries are the way to go. Do not try to make them up as you go because it will be easy to get manipulated by someone and hard to stay consistent with your boundaries. If you are not consistent with them, why would the person you are dating respect them? They will not take you seriously if they see your boundaries are optional.

- Think about what makes you happy and brings you peace. Those will be the boundaries you want to enforce with everyone you meet. Write down your boundaries below and practice them. The more you practice, the more natural it will become, and you will grow in confidence. What boundaries should you start implementing?

_____

_____

_____

_____

_____

15 Ways to Build Radical Confidence & Thrive

1-Do not engage in negativity

2-Work your boundaries

3-Love on you

4-Position yourself intentionally

5-Radically accepting what you cannot change

6-Connect with GOD

7-Exercise at least 3 times a week- movement is key

8-Important to work on finances

9-Establish safe community

10-Engage in therapy sessions as needed

11-Find your purpose

12-Pray, Wait, & Meditate on God's Word

13-Remain in God's love (John 15:9)

14-Be grateful for everything

15- Forgive and focus on the positive

Self-Love Through Physical Self-Care

- Prioritize self-care routines such as proper nutrition, exercise, and restful sleep.
- Engage in activities that bring joy and treat your body with kindness.

Describe your current self-care routine. How does it support your physical and emotional well-being?

_____

_____

_____

_____

Questions:

- What are some self-care activities you enjoy and find beneficial?

_____

_____

_____

_____

- How does practicing self-love through physical care help you resist people- pleasing tendencies?

_____

_____

_____

_____

_____

Stress-Relief Exercises for People-Pleasers

- Techniques include deep breathing, progressive muscle relaxation, and mindfulness meditation.
- Regular physical exercise can help manage stress and shift focus away from others' expectations.

Choose a stress- relief exercise and practice it. Write about your experience and how it affects your stress levels and overall well-being.

_____

_____

_____

_____

_____

_____

_____

Questions:

- What stress relief techniques have you found most effective?

_____

_____

_____

_____

- Can incorporating these techniques into your routine help manage people- pleasing behavior? Can they also improve your sleep quality?

_____

_____

_____

_____

_____

SPIRIT

Meditation on Self-Worth and Divine Love

- Meditate on affirming scriptures or spiritual texts about your worth and divine love.
- Reflecton how these beliefs can help you reject people-pleasing behaviors.

Meditate on a scripture or spiritual affirmation about your worth. Write about how this practice influences your self-perception and behavior.

_____
_____
_____
_____
_____
_____

Questions:

- How does meditation on self-worth and divine love affect your self-esteem?

_____
_____
_____
_____
_____

- In what ways can these spiritual practices help you maintain clear boundaries?

_____
_____
_____
_____

Aligning Actions with Personal and Spiritual Values

- Align your actions with your core values and beliefs.
- Ensure your behavior reflects your authentic self rather than seeking external approval.

Reflect on a recent decision you made. How did it align with your personal and spiritual values?

_____
_____
_____
_____

Questions:

- What are your core values, and how do they guide your actions?

_____
_____
_____

- How can aligning your actions with your values help you reject people- pleasing tendencies?

_____
_____
_____

Creating Peace in Relationships While Maintaining Boundaries

- Communicate boundaries clearly and empathetically.
- Practice balancing boundary-setting with understanding others' needs.

Describe a recent interaction where you set a boundary. How did you balance maintaining peace with enforcing your limits?

_____
_____
_____
_____

Questions:

- What strategies can help you create peace in relationships while maintaining boundaries?

  _____

  _____

  _____

- How can maintaining clear boundaries contribute to healthier, more respectful interactions?

  _____

  _____

  _____

Are you a people pleaser? Take the test below to get your results..

Instructions:

Reflect on your experiences and rate each item on a scale of 0 (never) to 3 (very often). This will help you identify areas that may be linked to people- pleasing behaviors and their impact on your well-being.

1. I feel the need to constantly seek approval from others.
   0 1 2 3

2. I have difficulty setting boundaries with others.
   0 1 2 3

3. I often neglect my own needs to accommodate others.
   0 1 2 3

4. I feel guilty when I say "no" to others.
   0 1 2 3

5. I worry excessively about what others think of me.
   0 1 2 3

CHAPTER 4

REPARENTING YOURSELF / ESCAPING CHILDHOOD TRAUMA

Reparenting yourself and escaping childhood trauma involves a holistic approach that addresses the mind, body, and spirit. This process requires understanding and challenging negative thought patterns, developing self- compassion, and establishing healthy boundaries. Physically, it involves reconnecting with your body through self-care practices, mindfulness, and somatic exercises to release stored trauma. Spiritually, it means nurturing your inner child through practices that provide comfort and meaning while seeking a higher purpose for your life. By integrating these aspects, you can heal past wounds, develop a stronger sense of self, and create a more fulfilling life aligned with your true needs and values.

MIND

Understanding and Addressing Childhood Trauma

Notes:

- Childhood trauma can manifest in various ways, from overt abuse to subtle forms of neglect.
- Reparenting involves recognizing how past traumas influence your thought patterns, emotions, and behaviors in adulthood.
- Cognitive Behavioral Therapy (CBT) and trauma-focused therapies help in identifying and reframing negative beliefs stemming from childhood.

Reflect on a childhood experience that continues to affect you today. How does this experience influence your current behaviors, thoughts, or relationships? How can you begin to challenge and change these patterns?

_____

_____

_____

_____

Questions:

- How has childhood trauma impacted your self-esteem and relationships?

_____

_____

_____

_____

- What negative beliefs have you carried from childhood, and how can you reframe them?

_____

_____

_____

_____

BODY

Somatic Experiencing Techniques

Notes:

- Somatic Experiencing is a body-oriented approach to healing trauma that focuses on releasing stored tension and trauma.
- Practices include slow, mindful movements, breathwork, and body awareness exercises to help the body return to balance.

After practicing a somatic exercise, describe how your body feels. What sensations did you notice, and how did they change during the practice?

_____
_____
_____
_____

Questions:

- How does your body typically respond to stress or trauma?

_____
_____
_____
_____

- What somatic practices can you incorporate into your daily routine to help release tension?

_____
_____
_____
_____

SPIRIT

Spiritual Reparenting Practices

- Spiritual reparenting involves nurturing your inner child through practices like meditation, prayer, and connecting with a higher power.
- Engaging in spiritual rituals can provide the love, guidance, and support you may have lacked in childhood.

Write a letter to your inner child, offering the love and support they needed during a difficult time in your past. How can you continue to nurture this part of yourself?

_____
_____
_____
_____
_____
_____
_____
_____
_____
_____
_____
_____
_____
_____
_____
_____

Questions:

- What spiritual practices bring you comfort and peace? Why?

_____
_____
_____
_____

- How can you use these practices to reparent and nurture your inner child?

_____
_____

How to Reparent

Reparenting is becoming our wise inner parent so we can:

- Quiet inner critic
- Explore/ validate perspective & emotions
- Cultivate compassion & patience

Four Pillars of Reparenting

1. Self-care: Focus on oneself
2. Loving discipline: Create new boundaries by making & keeping promises to ourselves
3. Emotional Regulation: Ability to navigate our emotions through new reactions
4. Rediscovering wonder/ awe: Learning how to play & being spontaneous/creativeness

Questions:

- What are some ways to relearn how to play?

_____

_____

_____

- What promises have you been breaking towards yourself?

_____

_____

- How much time do you think you should put aside each week to focus on yourself?

_____

_____

Adverse Childhood Experiences quiz or ACEs

The ACEs test, or Adverse Childhood Experiences quiz, consists of a series of 10 questions that help researchers and mental health professionals identify childhood abuse, neglect, and family dysfunction. Each affirmative answer is assigned one point for each type of trauma. The test is used to assess traumatic or stressful childhood experiences. The score also explains a person's risk for chronic disease. Think of it as a cholesterol score for childhood toxic stress. The higher your ACE score, the higher your risk of health and social problems. (Of course, other types of traumas exist that could contribute to an ACE score, so it is conceivable that people could have ACE scores higher than 10; however, the ACE Study measured only 10 types.)

As your ACE score increases, so does the risk of disease, social and emotional problems. With an ACE score of 4 or more, things start getting serious. The likelihood of chronic pulmonary lung disease increases 390%; hepatitis 240%; depression 460%; suicide 1,220%.

Children who experience ACEs and toxic stress may

- Have difficulty forming close relationships with others
- Have trouble keeping a job
- Have difficulty with finances
- Experience depression
- Be more likely to be involved in violence
- Experience early, unwanted pregnancies
- Be more likely to be incarcerated
- Experience higher levels of unemployment
- Be more likely to also expose their children to ACEs
- Have a higher risk of alcohol or substance abuse
- Have a higher risk of suicide attempts
- Have a higher risk of health issues such as heart disease cancer, lung disease, and liver disease

Ways we can prevent ACEs in children

1. Policy makers can work toward increasing financial security for families and preventing food and housing insecurity.

2. Workplaces can make their institutions more family-friendly and establish family leave policies.

3. Communities and policy makers can protect against violence by promoting anti-violence campaigns and education.

4. Professionals who work with families can teach positive parenting skills and teach socio-emotional learning.

5. Policy makers can promote a strong start for children by expanding childcare, preschool, and early childhood education options.

6. Communities can prioritize youth services, mentors for youth, and substance abuse recovery programs.

Take the ACEs test below.

ACEs TEST

Instructions:

Below is a list of 10 categories of Adverse Childhood Experiences (ACEs). From the list below, please place a checkmark next to each ACE category that you experienced prior to your 18th birthday. Then, please add up the number of categories of ACEs you experienced and put the total number at the bottom.

1. Did you feel that you did not have enough to eat, had to wear dirty clothes, or had no one to protect or take care of you? ___

2. Did you lose a parent through divorce, abandonment, death, or other reason? ___

3. Did you live with anyone who was depressed, mentally ill, or attempted suicide? ___

4. Did you live with anyone who had a problem with drinking or using drugs, including prescription drugs? ___

5. Did your parents or adults in your home ever hit, punch, beat, or threaten to harm each other? ___

6. Did you live with anyone who went to jail or prison? ___

7. Did a parent or adult in your home ever swear at you, insult you, or put you down? ___

8. Did a parent or adult in your home ever hit, beat, kick, or physically hurt you in any way? ___

9. Did you feel that no one in your family loved you or thought you were special? ___

10. Did you experience unwanted sexual contact (such as fondling or oral/anal/vaginal intercourse/penetration)? ___

Your ACE score is the total number of checked responses _____

Do you believe that these experiences have affected your health?

Not Much _____ Some _____ A Lot _____

Demographic Information:

Age: ___

Gender:

Male ___

Female ___

Transgender __

Declines to state ___

Race/ Ethnicity:

White/ Caucasian ___

Latino/ Hispanic ___

African American __

Asian/ Pacific Islander __

American/ Alaskan Native __

Zip code: _____

CHAPTER 5

RECOVERY WORK - BUILDING RESILIENCE

Building resilience is essential for navigating life's challenges and recovering from adversity. It involves developing the capacity to manage and respond to emotional experiences effectively through emotional regulation. This process integrates the mind, body, and spirit, providing a holistic approach to strengthening resilience.

MIND

Developing Emotional Regulation Through Cognitive and Behavioral Techniques

Notes:

Emotional regulation in the mind involves cognitive techniques, mindfulness practices, and fostering a positive mental attitude. These approaches help in identifying and restructuring negative thought patterns, increasing emotional awareness, and cultivating a resilient mindset.

Cognitive Behavioral Techniques

5. Cognitive Restructuring: Challenge and replace negative thoughts with balanced, realistic ones.
6. Behavioral Activation: Engage in activities that improve mood and break cycles of negative emotions.
7. Problem-Solving: Develop structured approaches to tackle issues that trigger emotional distress.

Mindfulness Practices for Emotional Awareness

8. Body Scan Meditation: Focus on different parts of the body to increase awareness of physical sensations associated with emotions.
9. Mindful Breathing: Use breath as an anchor to observe emotions without judgment.
10. Emotion Labeling: Identify and name emotions as they arise to reduce their intensity

Reflect on a recent challenging situation. How did you manage your emotions? Which cognitive or mindfulness techniques could have helped you respond differently?

_____
_____
_____
_____
_____

Questions:

- Which cognitive behavioral technique resonates most with you, and why?

_____
_____

- How can you incorporate mindfulness practices into your daily routine to enhance emotional awareness?

_____
_____
_____

BODY

Strengthening Emotional Regulation Through Physical Practices

Notes:

The body plays a crucial role in emotional regulation. Physical grounding techniques, understanding the mind-body connection, and establishing a daily routine contribute to emotional stability and resilience.

11. Physical Grounding Techniques
12. Mind-Body Connection
13. Establishing a Daily Routine

Describe a time when physical grounding techniques helped you manage your emotions. How did your body respond?

_____
_____
_____
_____

Questions:

- Which physical grounding technique do you find most effective, and why?

_____
_____

- How can you better recognize the connection between your physical state and your emotions?

_____
_____

SPIRIT

Enhancing Emotional Regulation Through Spiritual Practices

Spiritual practices offer profound tools for emotional regulation by providing comfort, guidance, and a deeper sense of purpose. Meditating on sacred texts, living out spiritual principles, and cultivating peace are key aspects of this approach.

Meditation on Sacred Texts

14. Meditating on God's Word: Reflect on spiritual teachings to guide your emotional responses and find solace during emotional turmoil.
15. Spiritual Reflection: Use spiritual wisdom to reshape thought patterns and manage emotions.

Living Spiritual Principles

16. Applying Teachings to Daily Life: Make conscious choices aligned with your faith's principles, such as choosing forgiveness over resentment or practicing patience in frustrating situations.
17. Bridge Between Spiritual Knowledge and Emotional Management: Consistently apply spiritual values to develop better emotional control and resilience.

Creating Inner and Outer Peace

18. Inner Peace: Achieve peace through practices like prayer, meditation, and self-reflection, which calm the mind and stabilize emotions.
19. Outer Peace: Actively work to create harmonious relationships and environments, such as resolving conflicts peacefully and practicing compassion.

How does your spiritual practice contribute to your emotional regulation? Reflect on a time when your faith helped you navigate an emotional challenge.

_____

_____

_____

_____

_____

Questions:

- What spiritual practice brings you the most peace and stability during difficult emotional experiences?

_____

_____

_____

- How can you more actively apply your spiritual principles to daily emotional challenges?

_____

_____

_____

- In what ways can you cultivate both inner and outer peace to enhance your emotional resilience?

_____

_____

_____

_____

Strategies to regulate emotions include:

- Identify and reduce triggers; Don't avoid negative emotions but be aware of them.

- Tune into physical symptoms; Pay attention to how your body reacts.
- Consider the story you are telling yourself; Change your perspective.
- Engage in positive self-talk and challenge negative thoughts.
- Make a choice about how to respond; Choose your reaction.
- Look for positive emotions; Focus on the good.
- Seek out a therapist; Professional help can be beneficial.
- Focus on the positive instead of the negative you see.
- Speak positive into existence.
- Try to calm down in the moment or remove yourself.
- Accept how you feel.
- Take a deep breath.
- Shift your thoughts and mind to find the positive in every situation.

Additionally, emotional regulation involves initiating, inhibiting, and modulating responses triggered by emotions. Remember that changing thoughts is easier than changing feelings.

CONCLUSION

"You Are Not Broken: Tools to Overcome Trauma & Thrive" is a profound journey that encompasses healing of the mind, body, and spirit. This holistic approach recognizes that the impact of abuse extends beyond just emotional scars, affecting every aspect of a person's being.

Through this course, we've explored various strategies and techniques to address each of these dimensions. We've learned cognitive techniques to reshape thought patterns, assertiveness training to rebuild confidence, and positive self-talk to nurture self-esteem. We've also discovered the importance of physical self-care, including practices like somatic experiencing and exercises for emotional release, acknowledging the body's role in storing and processing trauma.

Spiritually, we've delved into practices such as meditation on scriptures, living out spiritual principles in daily life, and creating both inner and outer peace. These spiritual elements provide a foundation of hope, purpose, and connection that can be crucial in the healing process.

Remember, healing is not a linear journey. It's a process that requires patience, self-compassion, and often professional support. Each step forward, no matter how small, is a victory. As you continue on this path, know that you are reclaiming your power, rebuilding your life, and rediscovering your inherent worth.

By addressing trauma through the lens of mind, body, and spirit, you are not just overcoming the past, but also laying the groundwork for a future filled with healthy relationships, self-love, and inner peace. Your journey of healing is also a journey of transformation, leading you toward a life of authenticity, strength, and renewed hope.

Thank you for allowing me to share your world during this healing process. With much dedication and practice, you will successfully get to the other side where there is freedom, joy, and peace! Allow me and my services to help you beyond this workbook. Visit my website to book an appointment with me and follow me on social media.

Additional Resources:

Website:

www.freedomfromyournarcissist.com

Https://ginatwumasimentalhealth.com

Facebook:

https://www.facebook.com/psychondemand

Instagram:

Https://www.instagram.com/gina_twumasi?igsh=MWJsdWk1MHhj bjF1NQ%3D%3D&utm_source=qr

TikTok:

https://www.tiktok.com/@ginat38?_t=8dz64I31vgs&_r=1

Podcast:

https://open.spotify.com/episode/6rWZPcwkX9BIFXYaUppWEz?si =0JIiIAWxSsWlPB6odbVVnw

Podcast:

https://open.spotify.com/show/0WTA5HHXQmPhWBVm5BAlOy?si =yY0P6rxcREiih1RiGKsXDg

YouTube Channel:

https://www.youtube.com/channel/UCfCVXJu6SyCC-608FwnNxqQ